To Palm...
Make...
...

This book belongs to a
new member of the
official Geek Club

I certify that I will embrace my geekiness &
I will be proud to be unique.

_____

SIGNATURE OF OFFICIAL GEEK

Attention folks, please get in line!
This cat parade will be divine!
It's our plan, our goal, to seek
the very best kitty geek!

*What is a cat's favourite colour?*
*Purrrrrrple!*

Which feline's sure to win the prize?
This year's winner will soon arise.
The kind of cat of whom we speak,
is the kind who has that geeky-tweak!

HOLE IN ONE

First up is the big kitty Bo.
His outfit's sure to win the show,
in bright plaid shorts and argyle tie,

he is a golf geek, my, oh my.

*What does a cat like to eat on a hot day?*
*A mice cream cone.*

ENZ
5283

I know that this may sound unique,
but I think my cat might be a geek!

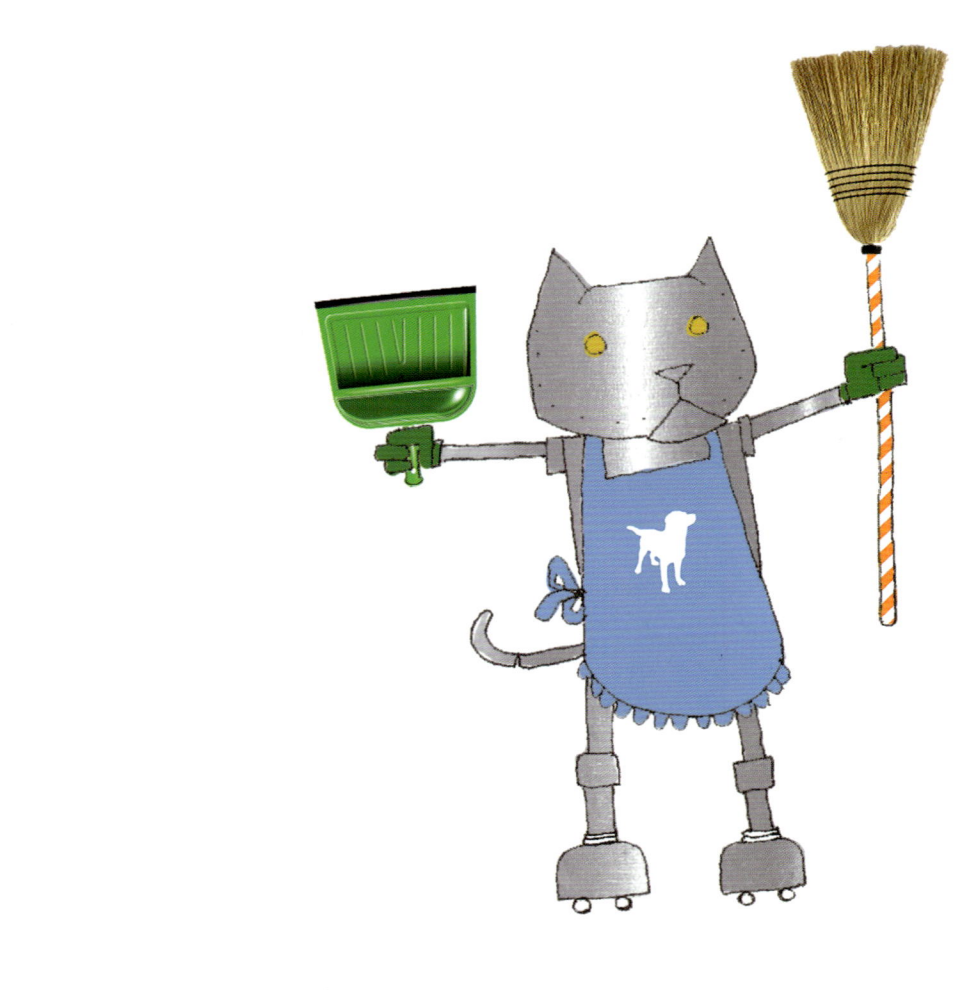

Emmy's an inventor,
she made that tiny Bot!
It cleans the entire house,
and babysits the tot!

*Why is the cat so grouchy?*
*Because he's in a bad mewd.*

clone 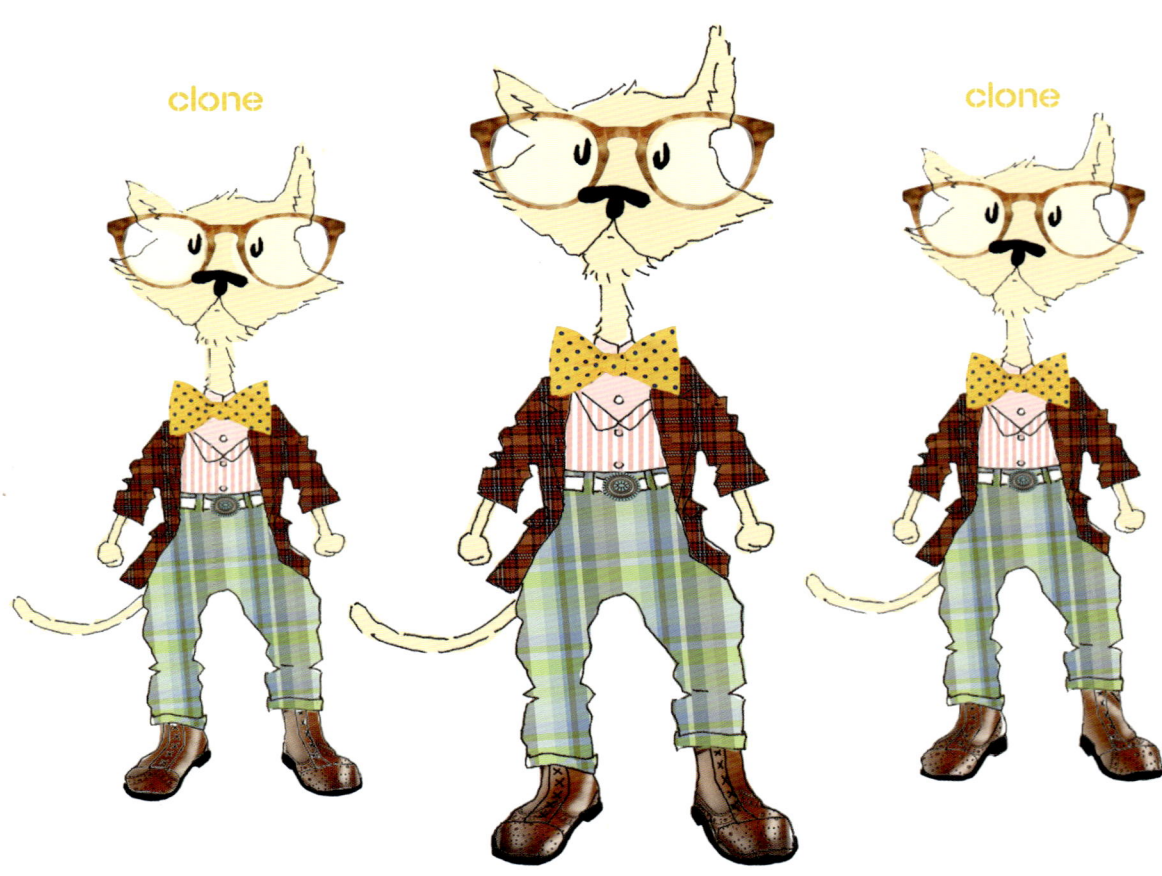 clone

*What do you call a cat that lives in an igloo?*
*An eskimew.*

Oh, you think your kitty's geeky?
Take a look at Pat.
High-water pants,
now he's a dapper cat!

His shoes with wingtips and laces
are sure to get attention.
Pat will take first prize
at this year's Geek Convention.

Maple's invention makes you sleep,
a better kind of catnap treat.
She made an app that you can use,
for peaceful sleep, it can't be beat.

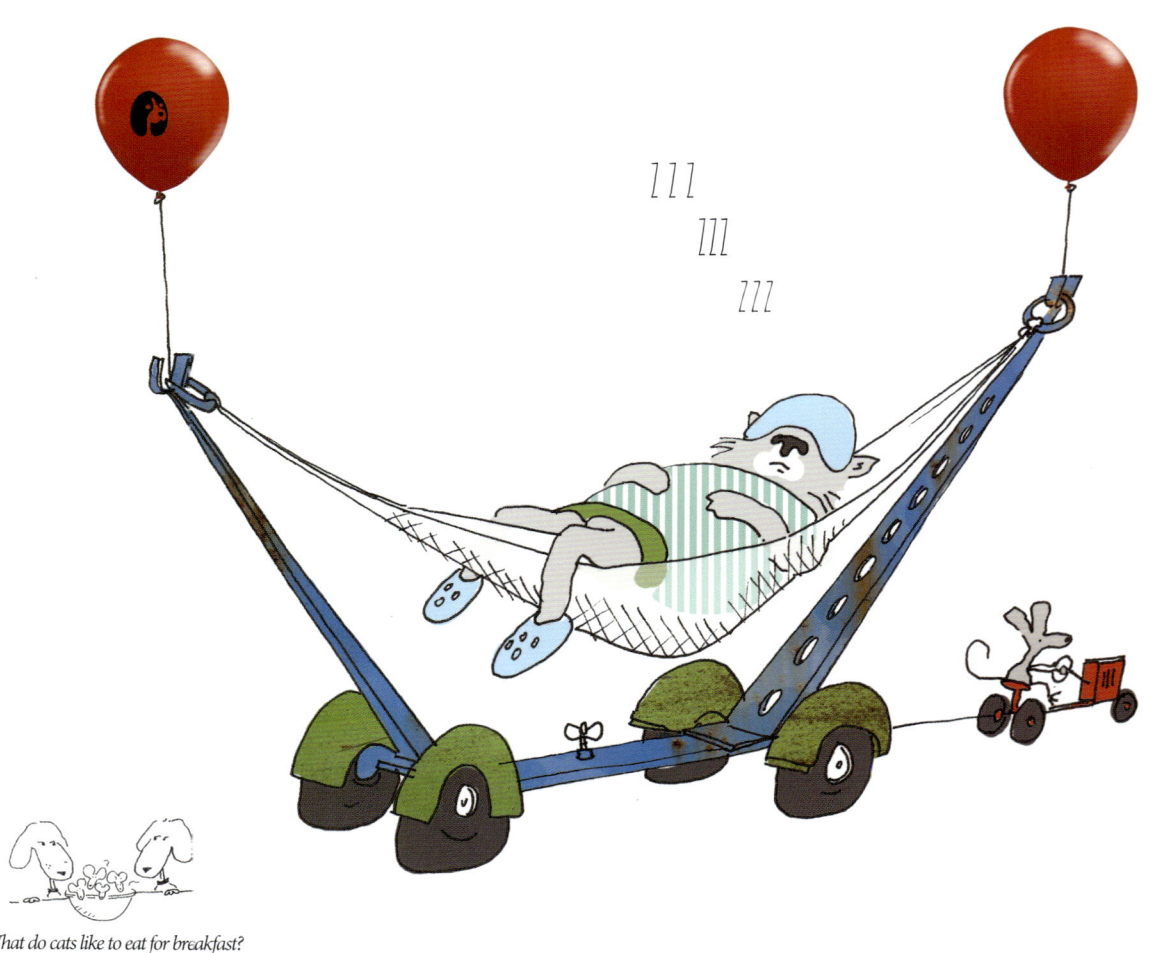

*What do cats like to eat for breakfast?*
*Mice Krispies.*

Mark's tail is puffed, his fur is up.
He's angry, someone let in a pup.
No dogs at all on his new apps,
"NO DOGS ALLOWED,"
it says in caps.

2 + 6 =

WING NUT

Now Allie Cat is smart and quick,
a laptop girl, her invention's slick.

Makes models of buildings,
a real math whiz,
think of any questions,
she'll take your quiz.

This is no rumor I'm trying to leak,
but I think my cat might be a geek.

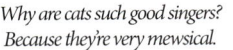

*Why are cats such good singers?*
*Because they're very mewsical.*

Well, Abby here's my mainframe geek,
she's like a mutt, I taught her to speak.
She programs games and then she'll play.
Determined to win, she plays all day.
She's so fancy she likes the finer things.
When you turn up the music
she sings and sings.

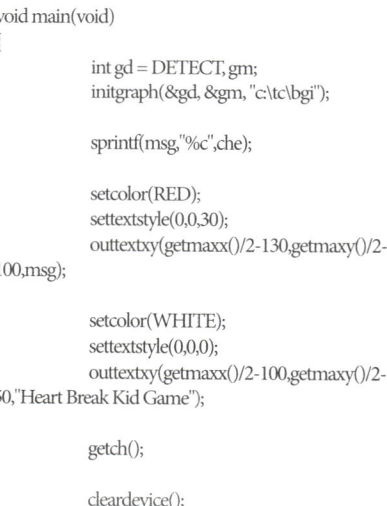

```
void main(void)
{
        int gd = DETECT, gm;
        initgraph(&gd, &gm, "c:\tc\bgi");

        sprintf(msg,"%c",che);

        setcolor(RED);
        settextstyle(0,0,30);
        outtextxy(getmaxx()/2-130,getmaxy()/2-
100,msg);

        setcolor(WHITE);
        settextstyle(0,0,0);
        outtextxy(getmaxx()/2-100,getmaxy()/2-
50,"Heart Break Kid Game");

        getch();

        cleardevice();
```

*What does a cat that lives near the beach have in common with Christmas?*
*Sandy Claws.*

My Mabeline loves make-believe,
she watches dragon shows.
Anything epic and fantasy
is where this kitty goes.

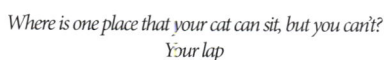

*Where is one place that your cat can sit, but you can't?*
*Your lap*

This girl's all about the geek-speak.
She's organized and wise.
Her attention to every detail
will help her win this prize.

Mozart plays piano, strings, horns,
and even flutes.
He wears a nice tuxedo,
and sometimes pinstripe suits.

He holds concerts for crowds
almost every week.
Mozart is a real pied-piper,
some say a music geek.

*What side of the cat has the most fur?*
*The OUT-side.*

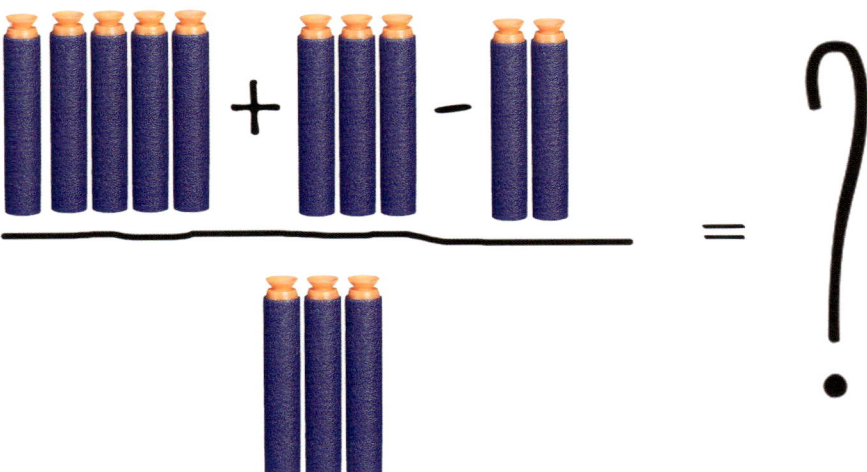

*What did the alien say to the cat?*
*Take me to your litter*

My Mittens competes, a "Mathalete."
He's an equation kind of guy.
But when he isn't doing math,
he's acting as a spy.

$$H(t) \, | \, \psi(t) \rangle = i\hbar \frac{d}{dt} \, | \, \psi(t) \rangle$$

My JoJo works on video games,
designs into the night.
She invents funny characters
and Kung Fu cats that fight.

*What looks like half a cat?*
*The other half!*

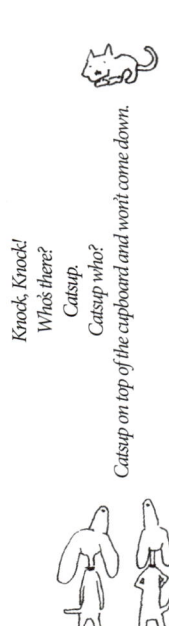

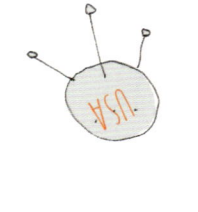

Banana goes to Kittengarden
where geeks and nerds all rule.
'Do unto others' all the time
when you kittens are at school.

She studies deep into the night
to pass her quizzes and her tests.
She will be a rocket scientist
nothing will stop her quests.

A+

1. THE PLANET MARS
IS_____MILES FROM
EARTH?

A. 105 MILLION MILES
B. 370 MILLION MILES
C. 249 MILLION MILES

*What do you call a cat that gets anything it wants?*
*Purrr-suasive.*

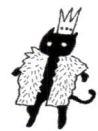

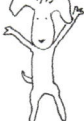

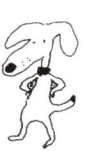

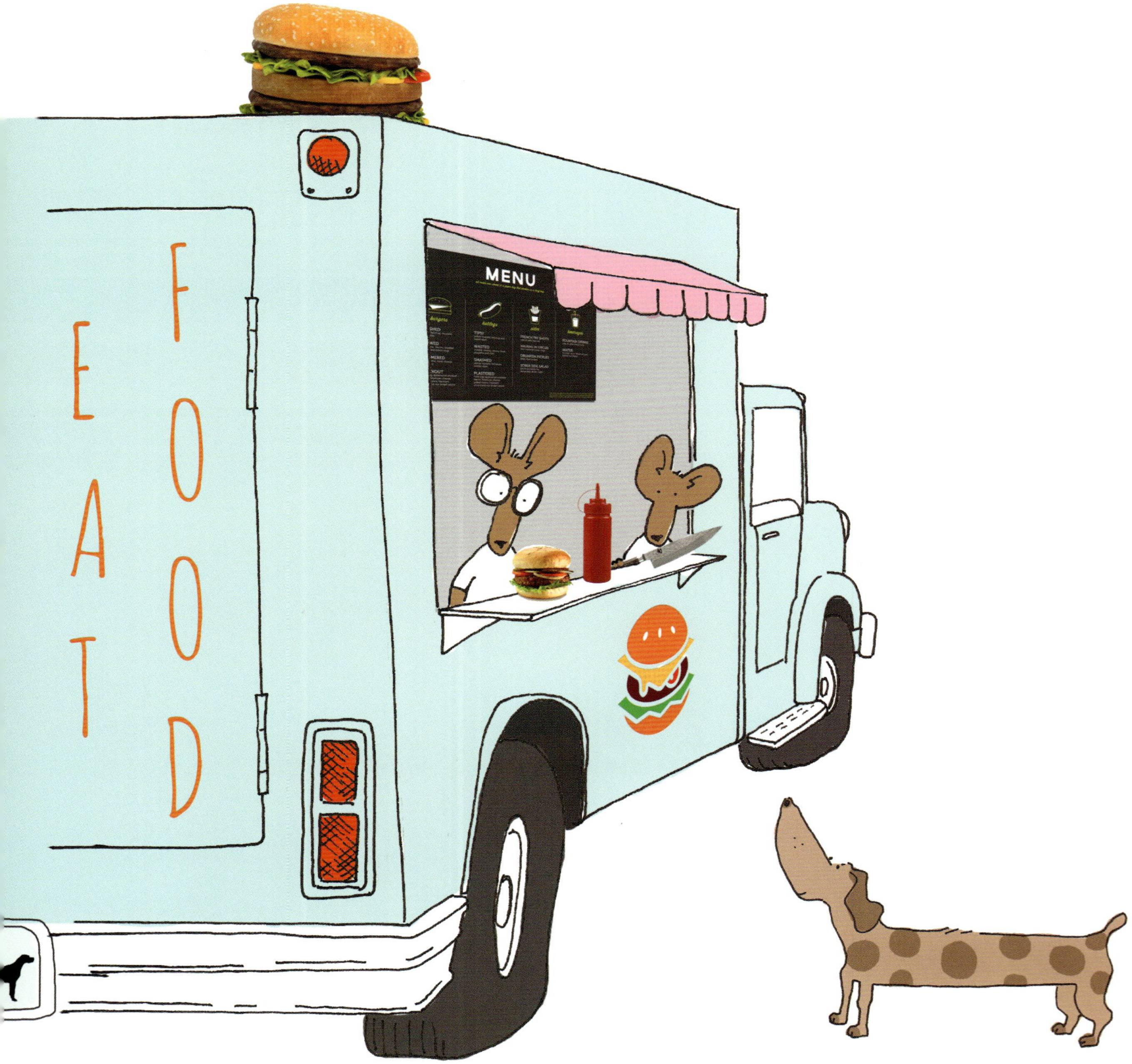

Tomcat Tommy's a foodie geek,
the kind who will be a kitchen boss.
He plans to own a big company
where he'll invent a secret sauce.

Johnnie is an astronaut.
He stares at the stars all night.
He wants to be the first cat on Mars.
Soon he will take his first space flight.

*What's a cat's favorite party game?*
*Mewsical chairs.*

LAB
QUEEN

Pickles is an internet star,
has many scientific shows.
Her videos show her gadgets
to keep cat-geeks on their toes.

Pwowie is a comic book geek
she is truly a fanatic,
argues day and night about superheroes,
and often acts erratic.

"My boy's the geek," Maple purred.
And Ember meowed to say,
"I think I must agree with you
on this fine and geek-filled day.
I know that this might sound unique
but I think my *girl* is the QUEEN GEEK!"

# Acknowledgments

BEFORE YOUR CATNAP READ OUR FOOTNOTE:
1. a digital technology expert or enthusiast ( a term of pride as self-reference, but often used disparagingly by others).
2. a person who has an excessive enthusiasm for and some expertise about a specialized subject or activity: *a superhero geek.*

I THINK MY CAT MIGHT BE A GEEK
Text copyright © 2018 by Justin Matott
Illustrations copyright © 2018, John Woods
Jacket design & illustration by John Woods
Design, illustration and Layout by John Woods
Interior illustrations copyright © 2018, John Woods
Jacket illustrations copyright © 2018, John Woods

Requests for permission to make copies of any part of the work should be mailed to:
Permissions Department, SKOOB BOOKS,
60 Falcon Hills Dr.
Littleton, CO 80126

Library of Congress Cataloging-in-Publication Data
**I THINK MY CAT MIGHT BE A GEEK** written by Justin Matott.
Illustrations by John Woods - 1st ed. p. cm. Edition
Summary: ISBN 978-1-889191-44-7 {1. picture book series. I. John Woods - ill. II. Tit e First edition
A B C D E

This book is dedicated to the coolest cats I know:
Ezra Arrow and Milo Aslan and Fudgey Ethan Matott; my favorite little Nerc Herd.
-Pops Matott

To contact Justin Matott regarding his work, please email him at
justin@justinmatott.com and/or visit his website at www.justinmatott.com

Contact John Woods through his website at www.johnwoodsstudio.com

Printed in China

*Why did the cat get pulled over by the police?*
*Because it littered.*

be PROUD to be unique and GEEKY.
Draw your portrait here:

_____
Your official geek name